THE
MALTESE FALCON

Hollywood Classics

THE MALTESE FALCON

Marie Cahill

SMITHMARK
PUBLISHERS INC.

Published by Smithmark Publishers
112 Madison Avenue
New York, New York 10016

Produced by
Brompton Books Corp.
15 Sherwood Place
Greenwich, CT 06830

ISBN 0-8317-4572-X

Printed in Hong Kong

10 9 8 7 6 5 4 3 2 1

Page 1: Sam Spade (Humphrey Bogart), Joel Cairo (Peter Lorre) and Brigid O'Shaughnessy (Mary Astor) gather round the object they have been searching for—the black bird.

Page 2: Humphrey Bogart as Sam Spade, Dashiell Hammett's hard-boiled detective, and behind him, a silhouette of the mysterious black bird that propels the action of the film.

THE MALTESE FALCON

CAST

Sam Spade	Humphrey Bogart
Brigid O'Shaughnessy	Mary Astor
Kasper Gutman	Sydney Greenstreet
Joel Cairo	Peter Lorre
Iva Archer	Gladys George
Effie Perine	Lee Patrick
Lt Dundy	Barton MacLane
The Gunsel	Elisha Cook Jr
Miles Archer	Jerome Cowan
Tom Polhaus	Ward Bond

Director	John Huston
Producer	Hal B Wallis
Screenplay	John Huston
Director of Photography	Arthur Edeson
Editor	Thomas Richards
Score	Adolph Deutsch

Based on the novel by Dashiell Hammett

INTRODUCTION

From 1931 to 1941, Warner Bros released three versions of Dashiell Hammett's 1929 novel, *The Maltese Falcon*. The first version was directed by Roy del Ruth and featured Bebe Daniels and Ricardo Cortez. In 1936, a second film made its way to the silver screen starring Bette Davis and Warren William under the direction of William Dieterle. The title was changed to **Satan Met a Lady**, a reference to Hammett's description of Sam Spade as a 'blond Satan.' These two films are all but forgotten. The third version, directed by John Huston, stands today as the best detective movie ever made.

Released in 1941, **The Maltese Falcon** was made at the height of Hollywood's golden era. It was a time of incredible creative energy, as superb films in all genres—romance, comedy, fantasy—made their way to the silver screen. The era saw the creation of film noir. **The Maltese Falcon** is the archetypal film noir, an exploration of the dark, seamy side of human emotions, of greed so strong that human life was valueless in the quest for the falcon. The film, like Hammett's novel, is driven by the leading characters'—Brigid O'Shaughnessy, Kasper Gutman, Joel Cairo and, of course, Sam Spade—relentless pursuit of the mysterious black bird—the legendary jewel-encrusted, golden falcon that was to be a gift from the Order of the Hospital of St John of Jerusalem to the Emperor Charles V in 1553. The falcon never reached Charles and for years its whereabouts were unknown, its true value undiscovered. Once its worth was revealed, lust for the falcon compelled men (and women) to search the world over for it, murdering everyone who stood between them and the falcon.

The Maltese Falcon was John Huston's highly successful debut as a director. Pleased with Huston's work as a screenwriter, Jack Warner of Warner Bros had promised Huston that he could direct **The Maltese Falcon** if he could produce a workable script. In spite of the two earlier box office failures, Warner was not taking a very big risk: the budget was under $300,000 and the shooting schedule was a mere six weeks. In what was perhaps his finest decision, Huston

took the dialogue almost verbatim from Hammett's brilliant novel—and this is where the directors of the earlier films had missed the mark. They had strayed from Hammett's novel, adding scenes of their own. A final stroke of genius on Huston's part was borrowing a line from Shakespeare to conclude the film. As the police detectives take Brigid O'Shaughnessy away, one points to the black bird, the object around which all has revolved, and asks 'What's that?' To which Spade replies 'The stuff that dreams are made of.'

As is characteristic of films of this genre, darkness and gloom permeate **The Maltese Falcon**. Most of the action takes places indoors, where stark lighting helps define the dreary mood. The mood created is one of shadows lurking in the dark, and in fact there are, as in the scene in which Spade slowly pulls the curtain away from the window to reveal 'the boy' that Gutman had tailing him.

Prior to directing **The Maltese Falcon**, John Huston had written the screenplay for another Hollywood classic—**High Sierra**, in which Humphrey Bogart was cast as a gangster with a soul. With **High Sierra** the seeds of the Bogey legend were planted; with **The Maltese Falcon** that persona was firmly established. By the time he was cast in **The Maltese Falcon**, Humphrey Bogart had starred in more than 40 films, many of them B gangster movies, with Bogart often cast as the villain. They were, by and large, films that are better off forgotten. These gangster movies accomplished their goal. Like the Schwarzenegger and Stallone action films of today, no one would ever call them works of art, but they served their purpose—they entertained the audience. Bogart did what the part called for, but the acting was of such a limited range that his talent as an actor lay dormant. Bogart once said, 'I've made more lousy movies than any other actor in history'; however, when given the chance to play a fully developed character—Sam Spade in **The Maltese Falcon**—he delivered a *tour de force* performance.

Opposite Bogart, Mary Astor played the cool, corrupt Brigid O'Shaughnessy. True to the character in the novel, Mary Astor's Brigid O'Shaughnessy is a clever actress. She is, to quote Spade, 'good, very good' at projecting whatever image is needed to get what she wants. Her skillful lying, combined with her striking looks, helped her achieve her unscrupulous goals. Astor's performance as Brigid O'Shaughnessy ranks as one of her most memorable. She played, to quote Huston, 'the enchanting murderess to perfection.'

Left: Director John Huston (in uniform) with his two leading stars—Humphrey Bogart and Mary Astor.

The cast of evil-doers is rounded out splendidly by Sydney Greenstreet and Peter Lorre. Under John Huston's masterful direction, each of these actors reached the height of their art. Every word, every action was flawless. In no scene is this more apparent than in the climax of the movie, as the leading characters cluster together in breathless anticipation of the falcon they have so long coveted. The usually polished demeanor of Gutman cracks ever so briefly as he realizes the falcon is a fake, that the supposedly jeweled bird is merely a black statuette. The camera captures his frustration by closing in on his penknife as it repeatedly scores the worthless surface. Gutman recovers almost immediately and philosophically sets out to continue his search of the past 17 years, taking the fawning Cairo along with him. The two of them walk out the door purposefully, Spade calls the police and—tough guy that he is—turns Brigid over to them. The movie ends as the police take her away.

At top: Mary Astor in 1920, as a young star of silent films, and *(right)* in the 1940s, at the height of her career.

THE
MALTESE FALCON

'In 1539, the Knight Templars of Malta paid tribute to Charles V of Spain by sending him a Golden Falcon encrusted from beak to claw with the rarest jewels–but pirates seized the galley carrying this priceless token and the fate of the Maltese Falcon remains a mystery to this day.'

And so begins **The Maltese Falcon**, the finest detective movie ever made. By beginning the film with this ancient legend, an aura of mystery is established before an actor even appears on the screen. The viewer is then transported to the present–San Francisco of the early 1940s–as the camera pans the Transbay Bridge that connects San Francisco with Oakland and the east (*right*). Except for Sam Spade's wild goose chase to Burlingame, a city south of San Francisco, all of the action takes place in San Francisco, whose foggy streets provide the perfect setting for solving the mystery of the Maltese Falcon.

That the film succeeds so well in capturing the mood of the city of San Francisco is a credit to John Huston's directorial skills. With a few nondescript facsimiles of San Francisco offices and hotel rooms, the Warner Bros' set designers had not given Huston much to work with. Nevertheless, he created a film noir classic that combines romance with a greed so strong that the characters are driven to commit murder.

The role of Effie Perine, Sam Spade's indispensable secretary, was played by Lee Patrick. Completely loyal to her boss, Effie understood Sam's moods and motivations. When a Miss Wonderly stops by the offices of Spade and Archer, Effie tells Sam 'There's a girl wants to see you. Her name's Wonderly.'

'A customer?' asks Spade.

'I guess so. You'll want to see her anyway. She's a knockout.'

An actress on Broadway since she was 13, Lee Patrick moved to Hollywood in 1937, where she was typically cast as a hard-bitten blond. In the 1950s she starred in two television series, *Topper* and *Mr Adam and Eve*, and in 1975 appeared in **The Black Bird**, a spoof of **The Maltese Falcon**.

Right: Miss Wonderly (Mary Astor) tells Spade her story. It seems her sister has run off with a man named Floyd Thursby. Desperately worried about her sister, Miss Wonderly has come to Sam Spade for help handling Thursby. The story, of course, is a complete fabrication, but Sam doesn't let on that he knows Miss Wonderly is lying.

Mary Astor was born Lucille Vasconcello Langhanke on 3 May 1906 in Quincy, Illinois. Her father, a strong-willed German immigrant, was determined that his daughter would be a star, and he encouraged her to enter a beauty contest when she was 14. The following year found her starring in silent films. In 1924, after a number of small parts, she won the leading lady role in **Beau Brommel**, opposite John Barrymore. From that point, until the mid-1940s, Mary Astor was a star. For the remainder of her career, she was in demand for character roles.

Mary Astor's credits include **The Beggar Maid** (1921), **Don Q, Son of Zorro** (1925), **Red Dust** (1932), **Dodsworth** (1936), **Prisoner of Zenda** (1937), **The Hurricane** (1937), **Midnight** (1939), **The Palm Beach Story** (1942), **Meet Me in St Louis** (1944), **Little Women** (1949), **A Kiss Before Dying** (1956), **Return to Peyton Place** (1961) and **Youngblood Hawke** (1964).

Right: In the midst of Spade and Miss Wonderly's conversation, Sam's partner, Miles Archer (Jerome Cowan), enters the room. Sam fills him in on Miss Wonderly's story, but it is Miss Wonderly's striking appearance rather than her story that sparks Miles' interest in the case.

Jerome Cowan's easy-going yet polished manner made him a natural as a supporting actor. Typically urbane and intelligent, and often sporting a pencil-thin mustache, he starred in over 100 films, including **Beloved Enemy** (1936, his first film), **The Goldwyn Follies** (1938), **High Sierra** (1941), **Song of Bernadette** (1943), **Miracle on 34th Street** (1947), **The Fountainhead** (1948), **Young Man with a Horn** (1950), **Visit to a Small Planet** (1960) and **The Gnome Mobile** (1961).

Overleaf: Eager to get to know the new client, Miles offers to handle the case personally.

This early scene reveals much about the characters' personalities. We learn, for example, that Sam has a sardonic nature. When Miles asks if Thursby could cover up by marrying the sister, Miss Wonderly replies that he has a wife and three children in England, to which Sam wryly comments, 'They usually do, but not always in England.'

Right: As the sunlight casts the shadow of their names on their office floor, Sam and Miles discuss the alluring and mysterious Miss Wonderly. In contrast to the camaraderie affected in Miss Wonderly's presence, they sit apart—a more realistic reflection of their relationship.

Though Miles jokes about Miss Wonderly—'Maybe you saw her first, but I spoke first'—Sam is unwilling to join Miles' attempt at humor and can barely conceal his contempt for him. 'You've got brains. Yes, you have,' Sam growls, as the scene fades to Bush Street—and Miles, the smile on his face suddenly turned to a look of horror as his assailant (unseen by the audience) pulls a gun and kills him.

They are partners, but not friends. Nevertheless, when Miles is murdered, Sam is duty bound to find the killer.

Right: Humphrey Bogart bore little resemblance to the character that Dashiell Hammett described in his novel as looking 'rather pleasantly like a blond satan,' but his personality was so ideally suited to the part it was almost as if Hammett had created the part with Bogart in mind.

After successfully working together in **High Sierra**, Bogart and Huston were eager to try another film. As a novice director, Huston appreciated an actor who knew his way around a sound stage and was willing to listen to his actors' ideas. Ironically, the part of Sam Spade was originally intended for George Raft, but he turned it down, probably because he did not want to work with an inexperienced director, and the part went to Bogey, much to Huston's delight. Off screen, Huston described Bogey 'as not particularly impressive, but something happened when he was playing the right part. Those lights and shadows composed themselves into another, nobler personality: heroic, as in **High Sierra**.'

Bogart, for his part, was glad to have the flexibility that working with Huston offered, but what was especially appealing was the role itself. Having long played the villain, it was, quite simply, the best part of Humphrey Bogart's career.

Right: This scene is rich in the atmospheric details that define film noir. As unidentified faces stare down at them, the two actors stand in the light of a lone street lamp, a dark shadow cast against the nearby brick wall. The grim and dreary locale of a deserted alley provides a realistic setting for a murder. The characters, especially Spade, are typical of the genre: loners disillusioned by life's ugly realities.

Here, Sam hastens to the scene of the crime, where Miles' body lies at the bottom of a hill. Police Sergeant Tom Polhaus (Ward Bond) questions Sam about what Miles was up to, but Sam can only reveal that Miles was working on a case. Considering the evidence—Miles was shot at close range, his coat was buttoned, with his gun safely in its holster—the obvious conclusion is that the killer caught Miles off guard. But Miles was too good at what he did to slip up on an easy tail job, so someone he trusted must have fired the fatal shot.

As Sam leaves the site, Polhaus, a friend of his, tries to put police business aside for the moment: 'It's tough, him getting it like that. Miles had his faults same as the rest of us, but I guess he had his good points.'

'I guess so,' Sam agrees unconvincingly.

Ward Bond often played the kind-hearted lawman or friend of the hero. Bond's career was launched when director John Ford's search for football players to appear in **Salute** (1929) took him to the playing fields at the University of Southern California. Ford recruited Bond and fellow player, Marion Morrison, better known as John Wayne, and liked the pair so well that he cast them as sidekicks in many of his movies.

It doesn't take long for the film's next murder to occur. Half an hour after Sam leaves the site of Miles' murder, Floyd Thursby is murdered—shot in the back four times. Thursby's murder casts suspicion on Sam, prompting Sergeant Polhaus and Lieutenant Dundy (Barton MacLane) to pay Sam an early morning visit (*left*). They know that Sam didn't go to Miles' house to break the news to his wife, Iva. Sam tells them he has spent the last hour walking and wondering—and he has no witnesses to support his story.

Polhaus gives Sam the benefit of the doubt, but Dundy suspects Sam has taken justice into his own hands and killed Thursby to avenge his partner's death. 'You know me, Spade,' he tells Sam, 'If you did it, or if you didn't you'll get a square deal from me and most of the breaks. Don't know as I blame you—a man that kills your partner, but that won't stop me from nailing you.'

Note how John Huston has once again used lighting to convey mood. Though this is an interior shot, it is as shadow-laden as the exterior shot on the previous page. The two policemen are in the dark (literally as well as figuratively), and Spade sits half in, half out of a shadow.

Much of the credit for creating the atmosphere is due to Arthur Edeson, the director of photography. Edeson, a superb black-and-white artist, had a long career with Warners, which reached its peak in the 1930s and early 1940s. In 1942, he was again teamed with Bogart, Greenstreet and Lorre for **Casablanca**.

Sam's code of ethics will compel him to find Miles' killer, but it doesn't stop him from having an affair with his partner's wife, Iva. Though Effie has done her best to keep Iva away from Sam, the next morning Iva is waiting for Sam at his office. They embrace, and through her tears, Iva asks him if he killed Miles so he could marry her.

Right: Gladys George played the part of the beautiful but untrustworthy Iva Archer. Born into a family of actors, Gladys George began her career at the age of three and paid her dues in vaudeville, in stock and on Broadway before heading for Hollywood. She appeared in a few silent films, but is best remembered as a leading lady of the 1930s and 1940s. Though on the stage she appeared mostly in comedies, in film she was typically cast in melodramas, most notably **Valiant Is the Word for Carrie** (1936), **The Roaring Twenties** (1939) and **The Way of All Flesh** (1940).

Overleaf: Spade receives a call from Miss Wonderly, who has left the St Mark Hotel and is now staying at the Coronet on California Street under the name of Miss Leblanc. The information memorized, he burns the message, as Effie watches, a look of concern on her face.

Sam's parting remark to Effie to have Miles' name removed from the door reinforces his calloused, loner image.

MF - 6

Left: Miss Wonderly has disappeared, only to resurface as Miss Leblanc. When Spade goes to see her, she confesses that her story was a lie, which Sam already knew, and admits that her name is neither Wonderly nor Leblanc, it's Brigid O'Shaughnessy.

As she did in **The Maltese Falcon**, Mary Astor typically played elegant, sophisticated, oftentimes malicious women-of-the-world. She was at her most venomous in **The Great Lie** (1941)—a performance that earned her an Academy Award for Best Supporting Actress, but it is for her performance as the ruthless Brigid O'Shaughnessy that she is best remembered.

Right: Sam listens intently as Brigid tells him her story about Floyd Thursby.

'How bad a hole are you actually in?' he asks her.
'As bad as could be. I'm not heroic. I don't think there's anything worse than death.'
'Then it's that?'
'As surely as we're sitting here—unless you help me.'

Brigid is indeed in trouble and is fearful that Sam will tell the police about her. But above all, she is cunning and manipulative. 'Now you are dangerous,' Sam tells her. Brigid, like the typical film noir leading lady, has always been able to control men, as she controlled Thursby, and regardless of her feelings for Spade, she intends to use him, too.

MF-17

35

Right: As this scene has revealed, Brigid O'Shaughnessy is adept at getting her way and Sam leaves, promising to do what he can.

Sam, however, is not like Brigid's usual victim. In turn frustrated and angry by Brigid's refusal to give him anything to go on, when he leaves, he is in command. He takes most of her money and tells her to hock her furs and jewelry. And he takes her key, telling her, 'I'll be back as soon as I can with the best news I can manage. I'll ring four times — long, short, long, short — so you'll know it's me. You needn't go to the door with me. I can let myself out.'

Most importantly, he knows that Brigid cannot be trusted. Nevertheless, he cannot stop himself from falling in love with her.

Above: Joel Cairo (Peter Lorre) visits the office of Sam Spade, explaining that he is trying 'to recover an—ah—ornament that has been, shall we say, mislaid. The ornament is a statuette, the black figure of a bird.' Cairo offers Spade $5000 to find the missing bird. This is the first mention of the black bird, but Spade knows that Cairo is a piece of the puzzle revolving around Brigid O'Shaughnessy.

Above: Although the novel was written a dozen years years earlier, it was as if Dashiell Hammett had Peter Lorre in mind when he wrote 'Mr Joel Cairo was a small-boned, dark man of medium height. His hair was black and smooth and very glossy. His features were Levantine.'

Previous pages: After his encounter with Joel Cairo, Spade goes to see Brigid at her room at the Coronet Hotel and tells her that he has seen Joel Cairo. In this scene, the expression on her face reveals why Mary Astor was so effective in the role of Brigid O'Shaughnessy. At the first mention of Cairo's name, Brigid is fearful. Then, we see fear mixed with caution, as she tries to figure her way out of this new tangle. She is, as Spade described her, good and dangerous.

Left: As Spade watches with an amused look on his face, Brigid betrays her unease by nervously poking the fire. Sam laughs at her, then kisses her roughly—and we see and feel the sexual tension of the two characters. In spite of his attraction to Brigid, Spade is growing increasingly frustrated with her. She has asked for his help, but she has given him very little information, and she has not said a word about the black bird.

She does agree, however, to talk with Joel Cairo, providing the meeting takes place at Spade's apartment. As they ride the elevator to Spade's place (*overleaf*), uncertainty and wariness is written on each of their faces.

While Brigid O'Shaughnessy is as unscrupulous and treacherous as Joel Cairo is, she is wary, for Cairo represents danger. In his pursuit of the black bird, he has tracked her down. For a price, Brigid is eager to be rid of the falcon, which has come to be a symbol of death.

Though Cairo does not know it yet, the Fat Man is also in town, adding yet another tangle to the mystery.

These pages: In each of these portraits, we glimpse the underlying sense of menace that Peter Lorre so convincingly brought to the many parts he played for Warner Bros. His rolling eyes, timid manner and mysterious personality were his hallmarks, but Lorre is perhaps best remembered for the roles in the films that found him opposite Sydney Green-street—**The Maltese Falcon**, **Casablanca** (1942), **The Mask of Dimitrios** (1944), **Three Strangers** (1946), and **The Verdict** (1946)—where his small build provided a striking contrast to Greenstreet's considerable bulk.

Right: At Spade's apartment, Brigid and Joel Cairo discuss the falcon — and Thursby's murder:

'What happened to Floyd?' Cairo asks.
Brigid shakes her head and replies simply, 'The Fat Man.'

Brigid and Cairo can barely contain their animosity for each other, and as their insults turn to slaps, Spade, once again, disarms Cairo. As Brigid quickly reaches for the gun, all further conversation is interrupted by a knock on the door, followed by the insistent buzz of the doorbell.

In this scene Bogey delivers one of the film's classic lines: 'When you're slapped, you'll take it and like it.' Cairo, however, seems to be of the opposite opinion.

The gritty realism depicted in **The Maltese Falcon** set the tone for the urban crime thrillers that came to be known as film noir, which translates as 'dark film.' The term was first used by a French film critic to describe the moody, down-beat character melodramas of the late 1930s, such as **Quai des Brumes** and **Le Jour se Lève**, but it soon was applied to American urban crime thrillers of the 1940s and 1950s, of which **The Maltese Falcon** was one of the first and the best. Later examples include **Laura** (1944), **Double Indemnity** (1946), **The Postman Always Rings Twice** (1946), **The Big Sleep** (1946), **Gilda** (1946), **The Narrow Margin** (1952) and **The Desperate Hours** (1955).

The characters of film noir, as exemplified by Brigid O'Shaughnessy and Joel Cairo (*right*), were ruthless and corrupt. Driven by lust and greed, the characters' desires led to their own destruction. As Sam Spade demonstrates, even the heroes were likely to be as disillusioned and cynical as the villains. Set against a backdrop of dark streets and alleys, sleazy hotels and dingy police stations, the world they inhabited was grim, dreary and fatalistic. These doom-tinged crime thrillers appealed to the post-World War II audiences because they dealt frankly with man's primal urges for sex and money, subjects which Hollywood, in the past, had had a tendency to treat unrealistically or not at all. Above all, they fit the mood of the times, when the world was disillusioned by war.

MF-302

59

Left: Humphrey Bogart's Sam Spade epitomizes the protagonist of the 1940s film noir. He is a tough guy, a cynic, a man with a closetful of vices, but despite his disillusionment with life, he adheres to a strict code of honor. As Sam explains to Brigid as he is about to send her over, 'Don't think I'm as crooked as I'm supposed to be. That sort of image might be good for business.'

Spade's philosophy extended beyond practical business concerns, as he tries to explain to Brigid: 'When a man's partner is killed he's supposed to do something about it. It doesn't make any difference what you thought of him. He was your partner and you're supposed to do something about it.'

While Joel Cairo and Brigid are at his apartment, the police pay a second after-hours call on Sam. An anonymous phone caller, whom we soon discover is Iva Archer, has informed them that Sam was involved with Iva and that's why Miles was killed, but as Spade pointed out, 'Your first idea that I knocked Thursby off because he'd killed Miles falls apart if you blame me for killing Miles too.'

Sergeant Polhaus is apologetic for disturbing Sam, but Dundy (above) is antagonistic. Barton MacLane, who played the part of Dundy, usually found himself cast as the heavy—a gangster, a Western outlaw, or the crooked cop or sheriff. In **The Maltese Falcon**, he was hard-nosed but generally on the right side of the law.

MacLane began his acting career on the stage, but he moved on to Hollywood, where he starred in some 200 films, mainly for Warner Bros. In the 1960s, he appeared in two television series: *The Outlaws* and *I Dream of Jeannie*.

Above: Hearing the scuffle inside Sam's apartment, Lieutenant Dundy and Detective-Sergeant Polhaus push their way in and discover a bloodied Joel Cairo. Dundy positions himself between Brigid and Cairo as he listens to Joel's version of what happened.

Right: A glimpse behind the scenes reminds us that this is only a movie, as the Warner Bros make-up artist works his magic and creates a beaten-up Joel Cairo.

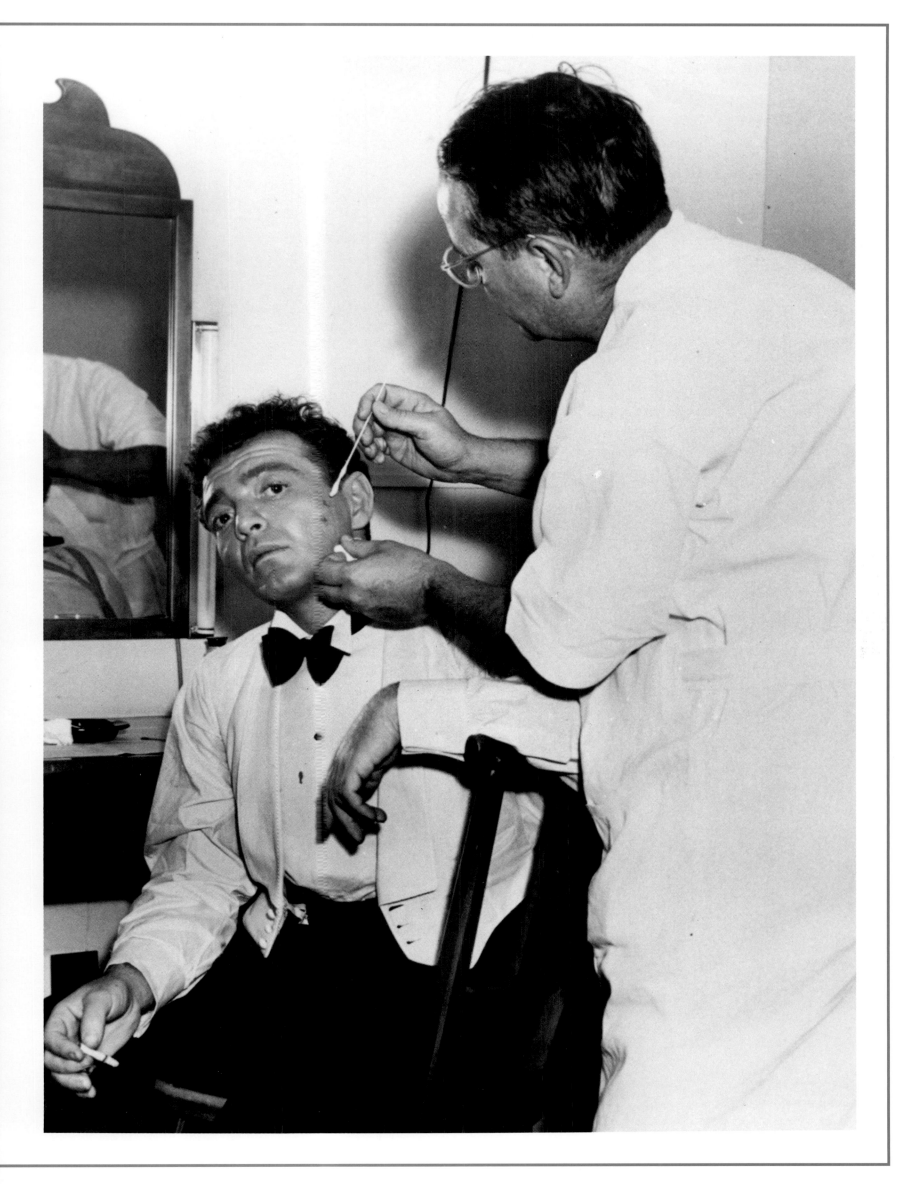

Above: The police would like to take the lot of them down to the station, but Sam concocts a ridiculous story about the scuffle having been a joke. Since Brigid and Cairo support his story, the police have no choice but to leave—after Dundy has taken a swing at Spade.

Right: The police have a few questions of their own for Joel Cairo, but with Sam's story they have no reason to detain him. After Cairo leaves Spade's apartment, however, the police catch up with him and take him back to the station for questioning.

Right: Finally alone, Spade presses Brigid for her story. 'What is this bird? he asks her. 'This falcon that everyone is so steamed up about?'

The Maltese Falcon was Bogart's first chance at playing the romantic lead. Though he wasn't the typical handsome leading man, Bogart played the romantic lead with aplomb. The chemistry between the two leading stars was so intense that John Huston paired them again the next year in **Across the Pacific**.

In subsequent roles, Bogart's characters would capture the hearts of Hollywood's most alluring leading ladies, from Ingrid Bergman to Lauren Bacall, whose heart he captured off-screen as well. After starring with Bogart in **To Have and Have Not** (1943), Lauren Bacall became Bogart's fourth and last wife.

Mary Astor, on the other hand, had long been established as a romantic lead, and she was even better known for her off-screen romances. At one point in her career, she had a stormy, well-publicized love affair with John Barrymore, and while going through her second divorce, Mary Astor's secret diary was used as evidence in the custody battle for her daughter. The diary scandalized Hollywood but also embarrassed a number of people in the film community by listing her various indiscretions, including an affair with George S Kaufman, the playwright.

Right: Spade confronts Wilmer, the 'boy' who has been following him, played by Elisha Cook Jr. A stage actor at the age of 14, Cook performed in vaudeville, in stock and on Broadway until he was 30. Once in Hollywood, his slight frame and shifty eyes made him a natural as the small-time gangster, often the fall guy. His role as the gunsel in **The Maltese Falcon** is one of his most memorable performances.

Cook's other films include **Her Unborn Child** (1930), **Two in a Crowd** (1936), **My Lucky Star** (1938), **Grand Jury Secrets** (1939), **I Wake Up Screaming** (1941), **Phantom Lady** (1944), **Dark Waters** (1944), **The Big Sleep** (1944), **Born to Kill** (1947), **The Killing** (1956), **One Eyed Jacks** (1961), **Johnny Cool** (1963) and **Rosemary's Baby** (1968). In the 1970s, Cook appeared in a number of made-for-television movies, such as **The Movie Murderer** (1970), **The Night Stalker** (1972) and **Mad Bull** (1977). Still going strong in the 1980s, Cook returned to the silver screen in **Salem's Lot** (1980), **Hammett** (1982) and **National Lampoon Goes to the Movies** (1984).

Right: Having survived the police interrogation, Joel Cairo returns to his hotel, where he encounters Spade. This scene shows Peter Lorre at his best. Though beaten up and exhausted, Cairo maintains his suave demeanor: 'Let's go someplace where we can talk,' Spade says to Cairo.

'Please excuse me,' Lorre replies. 'Our conversations in private have not been such that I am anxious to continue them. Pardon my speaking bluntly, but it is the truth.'

Overleaf: Effie Perine demonstrates her loyalty to Sam by agreeing to let Brigid stay at her apartment. On this occasion, however, Effie's woman's intuition has failed her. Effie is completely beguiled by Miss O'Shaughnessy's winning smile, and feels protective of her, even to the point of warning Sam that he had better not do anything to hurt Brigid.

Above: The mysterious black bird casts a shadow over everyone who comes in contact with it, including Sam Spade and his loyal secretary, Effie Perine.

Right: While in the midst of trying to solve the mystery surrounding the black bird, Spade must deal with Miles' jealous widow. As far as Spade is concerned, his affair with Iva Archer is over. Iva, however, has other ideas and she admits to Sam that she was the one who sent the police to his apartment.

Right: 'You're the man for me, sir, a man cut along my own lines,' the Fat Man tells Spade at their first meeting. 'No beating about the bush, but right to the point,' he says, giving the characteristic Greenstreet laugh.

Gutman tells Sam that he is the only person in the world who knows exactly what the mysterious bird is, while Sam claims to know the bird's whereabouts. The Fat Man doesn't fall for this bargaining chip and he refuses to reveal more about the black bird to Spade. Angered by Gutman's refusal to trade information, Spade throws down his glass, shattering it against the table. He gives Gutman until 5:30 pm to talk and then storms out of the room.

From the standpoint of size alone, Greenstreet's considerable bulk made him an ideal choice for the role, perfectly matching Hammett's description:

'The fat man was flabbily fat with bulbous pink cheeks and lips and chins and neck, with a great soft egg of a belly that was all his torso, and pendant cones for arms and legs. As he advanced to meet Spade all his bulbs rose and shook and fell separately with each step, in the manner of clustered soap bubbles not yet released from the pipe through which they had been blown.'

Sydney Greenstreet made his screen debut as the ruthless Kasper Gutman in **The Maltese Falcon** at the age of 61, nearly 40 years after he first appeared on the London stage as a murderer in *Sherlock Holmes*.

Greenstreet, however, had not planned on a career as an actor. He had originally travelled to Ceylon from his native London to make his fortune as a tea planter, but a drought forced him to reconsider his plans. Upon returning to England, he embarked on a number of varied careers, including running a brewery, until sheer boredom propelled him into acting school.

In 1904, two years after his debut on the London stage, Greenstreet toured the United States and spent the next two decades on Broadway and on the road, playing a wide range of roles, from musicals to Shakespeare. He spent most of the 1930s at the Theatre Guild with the Lunts, the famous couple of the American stage.

Although it has often been said that stage actors have a difficult time making the transition to the screen, Greenstreet, according to Huston, was 'perfect from the word go, the Fat Man inside out. I had only to sit back and take delight in his performance.'

Left: Having decided to reveal the mystery of the black bird to Spade, Gutman sends the gunsel for him. As the two are walking to Gutman's suite, Spade uses Wilmer's own coat to pin his arms and then takes his guns away. 'This will put you in solid with your boss,' Sam tells a disgruntled Wilmer.

In this scene still, we see the anger and humiliation that the gunsel (Elisha Cook Jr) felt when the Fat Man returns the gun that Sam Spade had so unceremoniously taken from him.

Off screen, Cook lived in isolation in the High Sierra, catching trout between films. When Hollywood wanted him, they would send a message via courier to his mountain retreat.

Overleaf: The air filled with tension, the Fat Man gives Sam the history of the black bird, telling of its incredible worth and explaining how his quest for it has been a consuming passion for the last 17 years.

Left: As a drugged Sam falls to the floor, the boy Wilmer savagely kicks him on the side of the head. Joel Cairo then steps out of the other room, and the Fat Man and his slight companion leave in search of the black bird.

As the unctuous Joel Cairo, Peter Lorre provided the perfect foil to Kasper Gutman. The pairing of the slight Lorre with the rotund Greenstreet worked so well that the combination appeared a year later under the direction of Michael Curtiz in another unforgettable Bogart film, **Casablanca**.

Director John Huston described Peter Lorre as 'one of the finest and most subtle actors I have ever worked with. Beneath that air of innocence he used to such effect, one senses a Faustian worldliness. I'd know he was giving a good performance as we put it on film, but I wouldn't know how good until I saw him in the rushes.'

Huston's praise for Lorre could easily have been applied to all the actors with whom he worked in **The Maltese Falcon**, for everyone in the film gave a memorable performance.

Right and overleaf: As these stills illustrate, the make-up department at Warner Bros did a convincing job of creating a nasty bump on Bogart's head, where the affronted Wilmer applied the sole of his foot.

Film star Marlene Dietrich once said that the relationship between the make-up man and the film actor is that of accomplices in crime. Indeed, she was right, for with a little sleight of hand a make-up man could make a beautiful woman even more glamourous, or he could create a terrifying monster from an ordinary human being. In the case of thrillers and melodramas, the make-up artist would make the audience gasp in horror as the heroes and villains exchanged seemingly painful punches.

Houston- 398 #
Makeup Still
Humphrey Bogar

Houston- 398
Makeup Stin #
Humphrey Bog

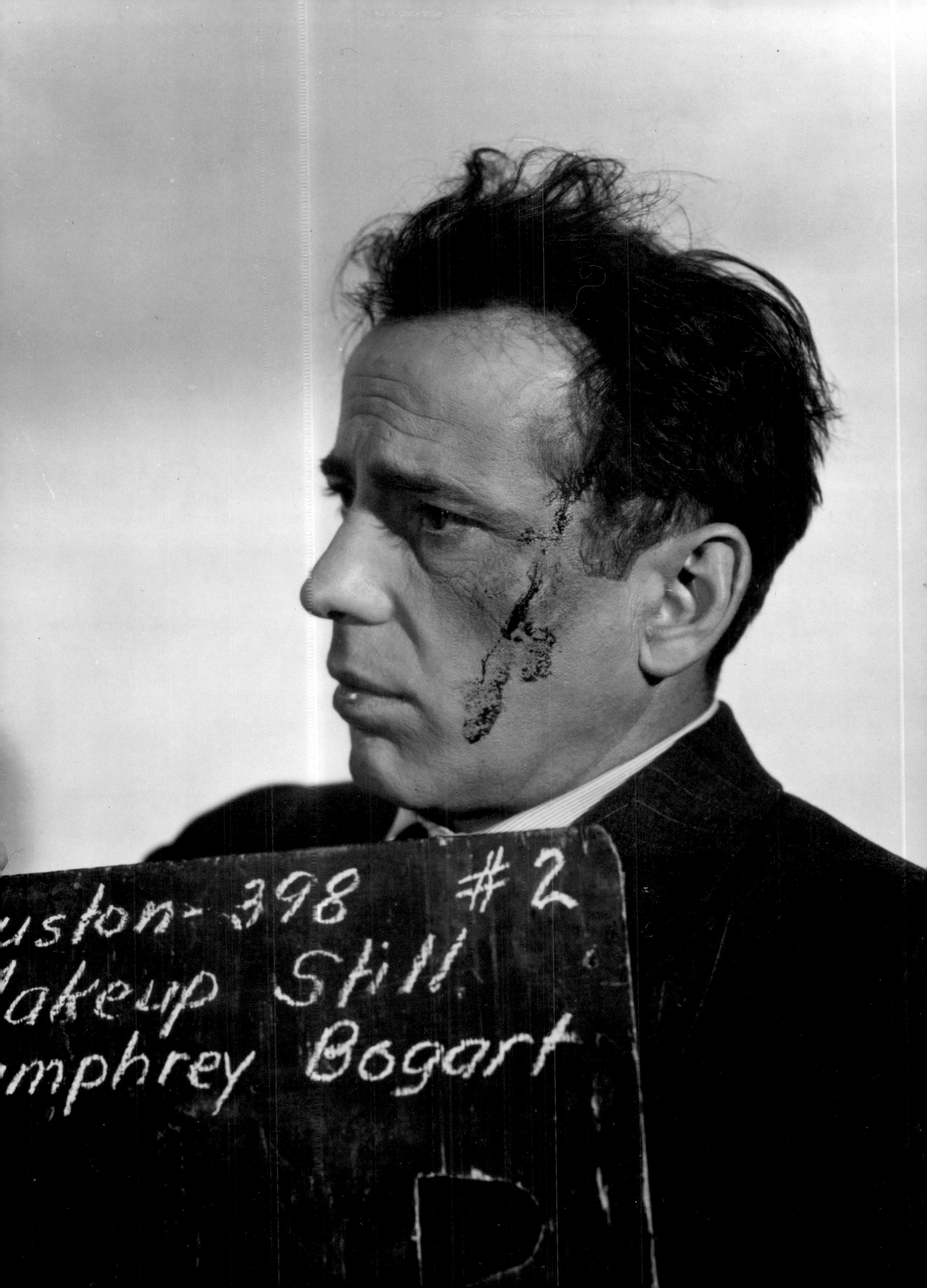
uston-398 #2
akeup Still
mphrey Bogart

Right: A dying Captain Jacobi delivers the black bird, wrapped in newspapers, to Sam Spade's office. In this scene still, Sam appears bitten by the greed that devours everyone who comes in contact with the black bird. Though a man lies dead on his office floor, his expression is clearly one of glee.

While they are exalting over this fortuitous turn of events, a phone call from Brigid O'Shaughnessy sends Sam racing down to Burlingame to rescue her, leaving Effie with the dead man and orders to call the police and tell them what happened—omitting the part about 'the dingus.' Sam takes the falcon with him, securing it in a depot box.

The bit part of Jacobi was played by John Huston's father, Walter. An actor with some 30 years' experience on stage and screen, Walter Huston would later have more substantial roles in his son's films, most notably **The Treasure of the Sierra Madre**, for which he earned an Academy Award for Best Supporting Actor in 1948.

The chase down to Burlingame was a ruse designed to get Sam out of the way, and when he returns he finds a frightened Brigid waiting for him (*above*). As the film races to its dramatic conclusion, the couple heads to Sam's apartment where, unbeknownst to them, the Fat Man and Joel Cairo are lying in wait for them (*overleaf*).

Right: In this portrait, we can see why Mary Astor was so believable as Brigid. Her striking beauty has captivated Spade, but her eyes reveal a woman of mystery and guile. As Sam tells her, 'It's chiefly your eyes and the throb you get in your throat….'

Left: The camera has effectively captured the tension that permeates the room. Both Lorre and Greenstreet have their eyes focused on Bogart, who is clearly in control. Lorre's stiff, straight-backed posture indicates Joel Cairo's anxiety as Sam leans forcefully toward the Fat Man, telling him that they have got to have a fall guy. The pressure Spade applies physically is equal to the force of his suggestion:

'Let's give them the gunsel,' Spade proposes, which Gutman categorically refuses. Later on, however, Gutman will relent and agree to turn Wilmer over to the police.

From this point on, all the action takes place in Spade's apartment. Huston had planned to film the scene in a number of cuts, but during rehearsals he decided instead to keep the film rolling and move the camera—which meant that the cameraman, Arthur Edeson, had to know the cues as well as the actors. The scene was shot in one take and, as Huston recalled, 'The suspense during the take was electric.'

And so was the final product.

Left: 'How do you feel now, precious? Nothing very bad is going to happen here,' Sam reassures Brigid, but she has good reason to be wary.

Before rehearsals began, Mary Astor and John Huston worked out the characterization of the amoral Brigid O'Shaughnessy. Her voice was hesitant, tremulous and pleading, her eyes full of candor. Here, we see Astor bringing Brigid O'Shaughnessy to life just as she and Huston had planned. Huston clearly was delighted with Astor's performance, for he cast her in a later film, **Across the Pacific** (1942), opposite Bogart once again.

Overleaf: In this scene, Gutman is testing Sam. Brigid hands over the envelope containing the money that Gutman has given Sam for his part in locating the black bird. As she gives him back the envelope, the Fat Man palms a thousand dollar bill and accuses Brigid of taking it. Although Sam knows that Brigid can't be trusted, he knows that she didn't take the money.

Right: At long last, the black bird—the fabulous Maltese Falcon—is within their grasp. Their eyes revealing their greed, Brigid O'Shaughnessy's and Joel Cairo's attention is riveted to the black bird and to Gutman, who gently caresses the falcon. In a moment, though, his penknife will scar its surface and reveal that the bird is a fake and that his long search is not yet over. In the ensuing confusion, Wilmer the gunsel makes his escape.

The directors of the earlier versions of Hammett's detective novel were compelled to make the story their own, adding and deleting scenes until the story differed substantially from Dashiell Hammett's novel. John Huston, however, knew better than to tamper with a classic. One of the reasons the film worked so well is that he had a good story played by good performers.

The film never wastes a second of time or an inch of space. Dialogue is brisk, and every shot is tightly framed. Huston had a perfect ear for dialogue, as he would prove again with **The Asphalt Jungle** (1950), a film which would win him high praise for its intricate handling of plot, atmosphere and characterization.

Though Huston was a novice director, his instincts were good. While he was willing to listen to his actors' advice, ultimately he was the one who decided where to place the camera to maintain dramatic tension, and where and when to move the camera to increase that tension. In short, he set the rhythm of the film and maintained it.

Overleaf: In this emotional denouement of the film, justice has finally caught up with Brigid O'Shaughnessy. A ruthless character, outside of the law, she has counted on Spade to protect her. But things have not turned out as she planned: 'I won't play the sap for you,' he tells her. 'I won't walk in Thursby's and who knows who else's footsteps. You killed Miles and you're going over for it.'

Right: Brigid is hit (literally and figuratively) with the realization that Spade is going to turn her over to the police for Miles' murder. Notice Astor's posture as she leans against the wall for support.

After a dozen years and twice as many films, Bogart finally played the hero, a character torn by his desire for Brigid and doing what he knows he must do. With this dramatic conclusion, the film rises above melodrama as Spade's situation becomes a summation of the dilemma facing the private eye.

Fifty years after its release, **The Maltese Falcon** still has the power to mesmerize the audience with its intriguing plot, riveting dialogue and vivid characterization. Truly a masterpiece, **The Maltese Falcon** was one of 25 films selected by the Library of Congress for inclusion in the National Film Registry. By virtue of their cultural, historical or aesthetic significance, these films have been deemed worthy of preserving in their original form for generations of film lovers to come.

Right: After **The Maltese Falcon**, Bogart successfully reprised his tough guy image in various films, most notably in **Casablanca** (1942), **To Have and Have Not** (1945), **The Big Sleep** (1946) and **Key Largo** (1948). In 1948, Bogart again worked under the direction of John Huston in **The Treasure of the Sierra Madre**, in which he played the part of the greedy and paranoid prospector. In the 1950s, Bogart demonstrated the range of his skill with widely diverse roles in such films as **The African Queen** (1952), **The Caine Mutiny** (1954), **Sabrina** (1954) and **The Barefoot Contessa** (1954).

Humphrey Bogart died in 1957, but the Bogey legend, as typified by Sam Spade, lives on. Remembered for his effective portrayals of the brooding, self-reliant cynic, Humphrey Bogart is the subject of numerous film festivals. With millions of fans, Bogey is admired around the world. Though he may have seemed an unlikely movie star, Humphrey Bogart made a lasting mark in history of cinema.

Left: Director John Huston poses for a publicity photo with part of his cast—Peter Lorre, Mary Astor and Humphrey Bogart.

John Huston was born on 5 August 1906 in Nevada, Missouri, a town that was, according to legend, won by Huston's grandfather in a poker game. He made his first appearance on the stage at the age of three and spent a good portion of his childhood travelling with his parents. After his parents divorced in 1913, Huston divided his time between the vaudeville circuit with his father, actor Walter Huston, and the racetrack route with his mother.

At 19, Huston made his professional stage debut in an off-Broadway production, but he was not yet ready for a serious career and soon embarked on a series of adventures that earned him a reputation as a colorful and impulsive character.

Huston's first stop was in Mexico, where he became an officer in the cavalry. Returning to New York from Mexico he again tried his hand at acting, as well as writing, but as a reporter for the New York *Graphic* his casual treatment of facts led to his dismissal. Huston then turned to Hollywood and screenwriting.

In 1932, Huston left Hollywood for London, reportedly for a screenwriter position with Gaumont British. Instead, he sang for pennies on street corners. He journeyed to Paris, studied oil painting, and did sketches of tourists to pay for his meals until he once again returned to New York, his passage home supposedly paid for by a Parisian street-walker. After working as an editor in New York, he left for Chicago, where he appeared in the title role in the WPA production of *Abraham Lincoln*.

In 1937, Huston again turned his sights to Hollywood and screenwriting, this time ready to establish a career. He successfully collaborated on several screenplays before Warner Bros agreed to let him direct **The Maltese Falcon**.

It was an auspicious directorial debut. **The Maltese Falcon** is considered by many to be the finest detective movie ever made, and many critics regard the film as Huston's finest work.

The cast of **The Maltese Falcon** clicked off screen as well as on. After the day's filming, many of them would go to the Lakeside Country Club for drinks and dinner. 'We thought we were doing something good,' recalled John Huston, 'but no one had any idea that **The Maltese Falcon** would be a great success and eventually take its place as a film classic.'

INDEX

Left: Humphrey Bogart will always be remembered as Hollywood's quintessential tough guy, an image that he originated in **The Maltese Falcon**.

Page 112: Sam Spade, cloaked in the shadow of the mysterious black bird.